Alexander Scriabin

THE COMPLETE
PRELUDES & ETUDES
FOR PIANOFORTE SOLO

Edited by

K. N. Igumnov and Y. I. Mil'shteyn

DOVER PUBLICATIONS, INC., NEW YORK

Published in Canada by General Publishing Company, Ltd.,
30 Lesmill Road, Don Mills, Toronto, Ontario.
Published in the United Kingdom
by Constable and Company, Ltd.

This Dover edition, first published in 1973, reproduces the
entire musical contents of the following volumes, originally
published by the Izdatel'stvo Muzyka ["Music" Publishing
House], Moscow:

A. Skryabin, *Prelyudii dlya fortepiano*, Vypusk [Volume] I,
1966, and Vypusk II, 1967.

A. Skryabin, *Etyudy dlya fortepiano*, 1967.

The titles, footnotes and other indications have been trans-
lated into English, and a new English table of contents drawn
up, specially for the present edition.

International Standard Book Number: 0-486-22919-X
Library of Congress Catalog Card Number: 72-93287

Manufactured in the United States of America
Dover Publications, Inc.
31 East 2nd Street
Mineola, N.Y. 11501

CONTENTS

ETUDES

Prelude, Op. 2, No. 2 (1889)

1) The composer did not designate the tempo; the prelude is traditionally played *Andantino*.

Prelude for the Left Hand, Op. 9, No. 1 (1894)

24 Preludes, Op. 11

№ 1

Part I (1888–1896)

1) Scriabin originally marked this *Ondeggiante, carezzando*, an excellent definition of the general character of the prelude. *Ondeggiante* was later deleted; *carezzando* remained in the autograph MS, but it too, apparently, was changed to *Vivace* in the proof stage.

Moscow, November 1893

1) In the autograph MS and in Belyaev's edition:

Preludes: Op. 11 (Part I), No. 1

6

№ 2

1) According to the composer's instructions, a brief caesura, with following *pp*, is possible here.

2) ___ (according to the composer's instructions).

1) *Accel.*
2) *pp* and *rit.* } (according to the composer's instructions).
3) See note 1.
4) See note 1.

Moscow, November 1895

Preludes: Op. 11 (Part I), No. 2

№ 3

1) This rest is not in the autograph MS; instead one finds:

Heidelberg, May 1895

1) The end of this measure, and the following measure, are corrected on the basis of the MS, where they are notated:

In Belyaev's edition:

In the Muzsektor's edition:

2) The MS has *f* instead of *d*.

3) The MS has *e* flat instead of *c*.

Nº 4

1) This prelude is based on a fragment from an unfinished Ballade in B Flat Minor of 1888:

The fragment is prefaced with the text: "A beautiful country! And life is different here!"

2) The original designation was $\frac{3}{4}$, subsequently altered to $\frac{6}{4}$ in the MS.

Moscow, Lefortovo, 1888

№ 5

1) In the MS, written as:

2) Scriabin originally wrote this passage differently:

1) In the MS:

2) In the MS:

3) Here Scriabin thought it possible to add the fifth in the bass, thus:

Amsterdam, 1896

Preludes: Op. 11 (Part I), No. 5

№ 6

Kiev, 1889

Preludes: Op. 11 (Part 1), No. 6

№ 7

Part II (1894–1896)

Allegro assai M.M. ♩. = 152

1) Here, according to the composer's instructions, a brief
caesura is possible.

*) Corrected on the basis of the MS; some editions print *b* here.

Moscow, 1895

1) See note 1.

Preludes: Op. 11 (Part II), No. 7

№ 8

Allegro agitato M.M. ♩=132

1) Originally this *p* was not in the MS; the composer himself did not consider it obligatory and often omitted it, beginning the prelude *f* .

1) This *dim.* is not in the MS, and the composer usually did not observe it, but played *subito* **pp** in the fourth measure of this line.

2) The MS here has a ⌢ over the bar line.

3) Originally there was one more measure here, namely:

Paris, 1896

Preludes: Op. 11 (Part II), No. 8

№ 9

Moscow, November 1895

Preludes: Op. 11 (Part II), No. 9

№ 10

Moscow, 1894

Preludes: Op. 11 (Part II), No. 10

№ 11

Allegro assai M.M. ♪ = 126

1) *rit.* (according to the composer's instructions).

rit.

cresc. con passione

Moscow, November 1895

1) The MS here has a *rit.* leading to a slower tempo: starting with the third measure of this line,
M.M. ♪ =100 (in accordance with the MS).

2) According to the composer's instructions, a brief caesura with following *p* is possible
before the *g* sharp.

Preludes: Op. 11 (Part II), No. 11

№ 12

Andante M.M ♪ = 126

1) According to the composer's instructions, the fermatas need not be of equal length.

2) This *pp* is not in the MS; the following measure (third from the end) is marked *sotto voce* and only just before the very end (in the next-to-last measure) is there a *pp*.

Vitznau, June 1895

Preludes: Op. 11 (Part II), No. 12

№ 13

Lento M.M. ♩=76

1) *rit.* (according to the composer's instructions).
2) Originally this measure was repeated.

3) As originally set down, the ending of the prelude was:

Moscow, 1895

26

№ 14 [1]

1) The title leaf of the MS of this prelude bears the following inscription, written with great care, most likely not by Scriabin himself: "A Monsieur J. Wysman. Souvenir amicale [sic]."

Preludes: Op. 11 (Part III), No. 14

№ 15

Moscow, 1895

1) *rit.* }
2) - - } according to the composer's instructions.

1) In the MS:

2) In the MS and in Belyaev's edition:

3) *accel.* }
4) *ten.* } according to the composer's instructions.

Dresden, 1895

Preludes: Op. 11 (Part III), No. 14

№ 16

Misterioso M.M. ♪ = 160-168

sotto voce

1) Apparently these three sixteenth notes were not originally in the MS: Scriabin wrote them in with a different ink, with a barely legible mark in front of the last sixteenth note in the left hand. Belyaev's edition prints a natural sign here, thus: , but this is dubious.

Preludes: Op. 11 (Part III), No. 16

Moscow, November 1895

№ 17

Vitznau, June 1895

1) The meter designation $\frac{6}{4}$ follows the Muzsektor edition; the MS and Belyaev's edition have $\frac{3}{2}$.

2) This *accel.* is not in the MS; Scriabin himself began it a bit later on, and moved at once into the *rit.*

№ 18

Allegro agitato M. M. ♩ = 138

1) In the MS, the first quarter-beat of this measure is marked *sf*, the second *p*.

2) The MS has *sf* here.

Vitznau, June 1895

34

№ 19

1) *pp* } according to the composer's instructions.
2) ... }

Preludes: Op. 11 (Part IV), No. 19

Heidelberg, 1895

1) *accel.* (according to the composer's instructions).
2) Originally there was one more measure here, like the preceding one.

Preludes: Op. 11 (Part IV), No. 19

№ 20

1) The composer did not play this triplet evenly: he lengthened the second eighth note (as if dotting it), thus turning the last eighth note of the triplet into a sixteenth. In general, this was quite characteristic of his manner of playing.

Moscow, 1895

№ 21

Andante M.M. ♩=108

1) In the MS, this *e* flat is an *e* and the prelude ends in the major mode.

Moscow, 1895

1) - - -
2) *p* and *rit.*
3) *rit.* } according to the composer's instructions.
4) The composer himself began this **pp** a little later: starting with the third fourth note.

Preludes: Op. 11 (Part IV), No. 21

№ 22

1) Corrected on the basis of the MS; all editions of Scriabin's works give *a* flat here.

2) In this passage the composer thought it possible to omit both the *p* and the *pp*, and to play the last chord of the measure *forte*; the *pp* did not enter until the following measure, in which the chord with the fermata (*pp*) ought to sound "like an echo" of the preceding chord.

Paris, 1896

Nº 23

Vitznau, 1895

Preludes: Op. 11 (Part IV), No. 23

№ 24

Heidelberg, 1895

Preludes: Op. 11 (Part IV), No. 24

Six Preludes, Op. 13 (1895)

№ 1

* The MS originally showed a sharp in front of the *c*.

** Corrected on the basis of the MS; all editions print [image] here.

Moscow, November 1895

* In the MS there is a natural sign instead of the flat sign, and over the note there is a question mark, most likely not in Scriabin's hand.

** In the MS there is a natural sign instead of the flat sign.

Preludes: Op. 13, No. 1

№ 2

accel. sin al fine

Presto

Moscow, 1895

* The MS has *sf* here.

** As originally set down, the prelude ended:

№ 3

Andante M.M. ♩ = 52-54-56

Moscow, November 1895

№ 4

Allegro M.M. ♩ = 92

poco accel. rallent.

Più vivo

accel.

stretto

Moscow, November 1895

Preludes: Op. 13, No. 4

№ 5

Moscow, 1895

* Originally this measure was repeated.

** In the MS, the prelude ended:

Preludes: Op. 13, No. 5

№ 6

Presto

mp

Preludes: Op. 13, No. 6

Moscow, 1895

* In the MS:

** In the MS the final chords are not tied.

Preludes: Op. 13, No. 6

Five Preludes, Op. 15 (1895–1896)

№ 1

Moscow, 1895

Preludes: Op. 15, No. 1

№ 2

* Scriabin originally wrote *Agitato*. Later this was deleted and replaced by *Vivo*.

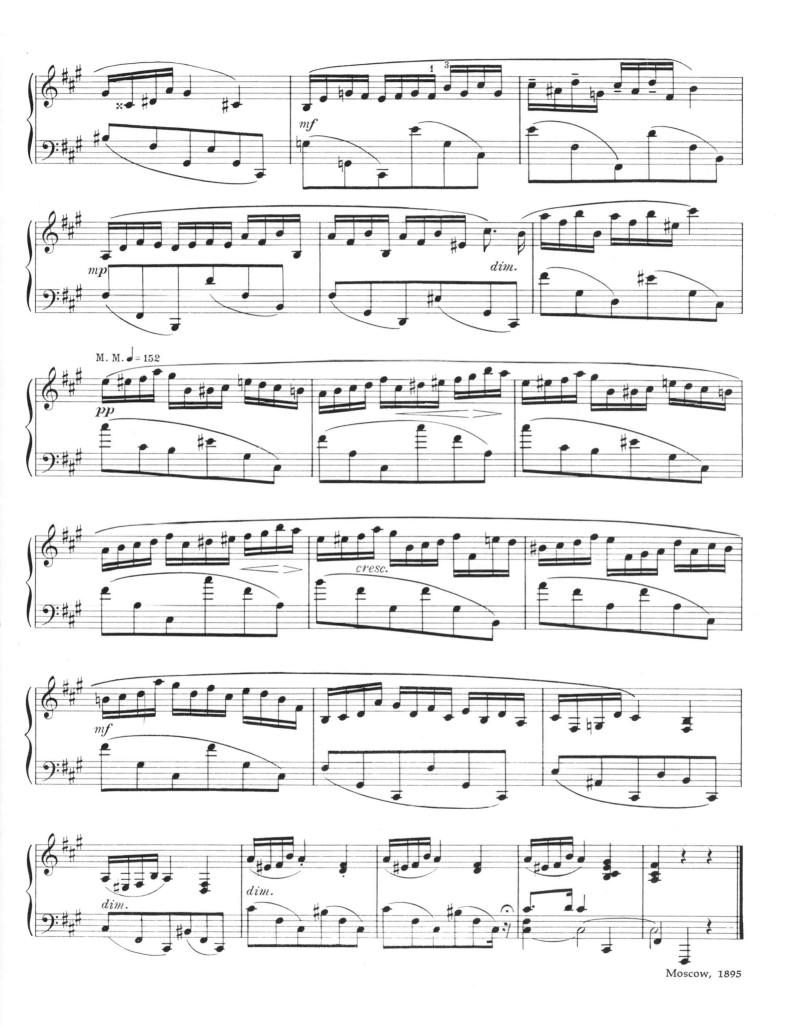

M. M. ♩ = 152

Moscow, 1895

Preludes: Op. 15, No. 2

№ 3

Allegro assai M.M. ♩· = 120 - 126

*) *mf*

cresc.

f

dim.

simile

sim.

cresc.

f

mf

p

cresc.

* The MS has *f* instead of *mf*.

Preludes: Op. 15, No. 3

Moscow, 1895

*) ?

** The MS has: , but this is probably a slip of the pen; the e should be deleted instead of the c sharp.

*** In the MS, the prelude ends:

№4

№ 5

Andante M. M. $\flat$ *) = 160 - 152

rubato

Heidelberg, 1895

* Corrected on the basis of the MS; all editions give $\flat \cdot$ = 160 - 152 , which is in fundamental contradiction to the composer's intention.

Five Preludes, Op. 16 (1894–1895)

№ 1

Moscow, January 1894

Preludes: Op. 16, No. 1

№ 2

Allegro M.M. ♩ = 80

pp

cresc.

dim.

pp

* Corrected on the basis of an indication of Scriabin himself. In the MS and in Belyaev's edition:

Vitznau, June 1895

* In the MS this passage is written:

** In the MS this passage is written:

Preludes: Op. 16, No. 2

№ 3

Andante cantabile M.M. ♩ = 63

* In the MS, 32 measures are deleted here.

Moscow, 1894

Preludes: Op. 16, No. 3

№ 4

Lento M.M. ♩=44

p sotto voce

cresc.

mf

dim.

p. *pp*

ppp

St. Petersburg, 1895

* Thus in the MS and all editions, but it possibly should be:

Preludes: Op. 16, No. 4

№ 5

Seven Preludes, Op. 17 (1895–1896)

№ 1

Paris, February 1896

Preludes: Op. 17, No. 1

№ 2

Paris, 1896

Preludes: Op. 17, No. 2

№ 3

rit.   a tempo

rubato

cresc.

mf ———————→ ppp

pp

ppp

smorz.

Paris, February 1896

Preludes: Op. 17, No. 3

№ 4

Moscow, November 1895

Preludes: Op. 17, No. 4

№ 5

*In the MS and in Belyaev's edition: ⎯, but this is doubtless a slip of the pen.

Preludes: Op. 17, No. 5

Heidelberg, 1895

Preludes: Op. 17, No. 5

№ 6

Moscow, 1895

№ 7

* The MS has $\frac{3}{4}$ instead of $\frac{9}{8}$.

84

St. Petersburg, April 1895

Preludes: Op. 17, No. 7

Four Preludes, Op. 22 (1897)

№ 1

№ 2

№ 3

Allegretto M.M. ♩ = 152

Preludes: Op. 22, No. 3

№ 4

Andantino ♩ = 160

Two Preludes, Op. 27 (1900)

№ 1

Preludes: Op. 27, No. 1

№ 2

Andante ♩=96

Four Preludes, Op. 31 (1903)
№ 1

Preludes: Op. 31, No. 1

№2

№ 3

№ 4

Lento ♩=54

Four Preludes, Op. 33 (1903)

№ 1

№ 2

Vagamente ♩.=58

*)?

№ 3

* Thus in all editions, but it possibly should be:

№ 4

Ardito, bellicoso ♩ = 152–160

Three Preludes, Op. 35 (1903)
№ 1

Preludes: Op. 35, No. 1

№ 2

№ 3

Scherzoso ♩.=126

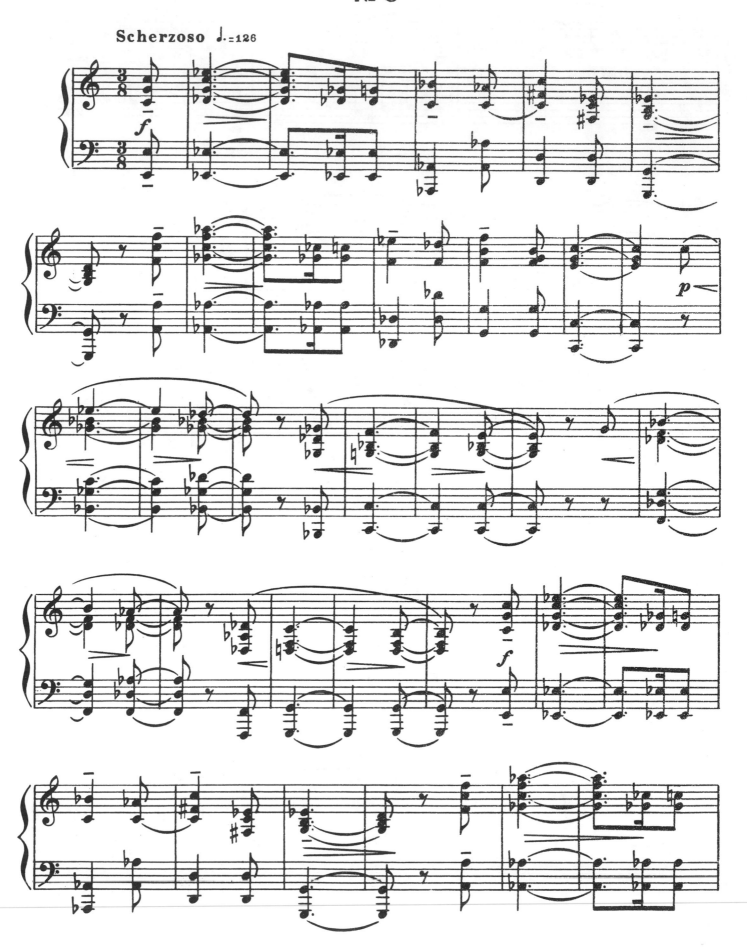

Preludes: Op. 35, No. 3

Preludes: Op. 35, No. 3

Four Preludes, Op. 37 (1903)
№ 1

Preludes: Op. 37, No. 1

№ 2

Maestoso, fiero ♩.= 76-80

114

Preludes: Op. 37, No. 2

№ 3

Preludes: Op. 37, No. 3

№ 4

Irato impetuoso ♩ = 72-76

118

Preludes: Op. 37, No. 4

Four Preludes, Op. 39 (1903)
№ 1

Preludes: Op. 39, No. 1

ritardando molto

Preludes: Op. 39, No. 1

№2

№ 3

Languido ♩ 40

pp
legato

cresc.

ritard.   a tempo

mf

pp carezzando

pp

ritard.   a tempo

mf

pp carezzando

Preludes: Op. 39, No. 3

№ 4

Prelude, Op. 45, No. 3 (1904)

Preludes: Op. 45, No. 3

Four Preludes, Op. 48 (1905)

№ 1

Impetuoso fiero ♩=120

№ 2

№ 3

Capricciosamente affannato ♩=144-152

Preludes: Op. 48, No. 3

№ 4

Festivamente ♩=88-100

Prelude, Op. 49, No. 2 (1905)

Prelude, Op. 51, No. 2 (1906)

Prelude, Op. 56, No. 1

Violent, très accentué

Preludes: Op. 56, No. 1

Prelude, Op. 59, No. 2 (1910)

Sauvage, belliqueux

138

avec défi

Maximum Likelihood

Two Preludes, Op. 67 (1912–1913)
№ 1

Andante

molto accel.

molto ritard.

Preludes: Op. 67, No. 1

№ 2

Presto

Preludes: Op. 67, No. 2

Five Preludes, Op. 74 (1914)

№ 1

Douloureux, déchirant

144

№ 2

Très lent, contemplatif

Preludes: Op. 74, No. 2

№ 3

Allegro drammatico

Preludes: Op. 74, No. 3

№4

Lent, vague, indécis

148

Preludes: Op. 74, No. 4

№ 5

Fier, belliqueux

impérieux

Preludes: Op. 74, No. 5

Etude, Op. 2, No. 1 (1887)*⁾

Andante

* The year of composition given here is based on the chronological list of juvenilia drawn up by Scriabin himself in 1889.

Etudes: Op. 2, No. 1

1)

Twelve Etudes, Op. 8 (1894)

№ 1

Part I

1) These etudes were revised several times before their appearance in print in 1895. Nos. 7, 8, 11 and 12 were especially heavily revised.

2) *pp*   }
3) *accel.*   } according to the composer's instructions.

Etudes: Op. 8 (Part I), No. 1

4) The author thought a *dim.* was possible here, with a *pp* instead of *sf* on the first fourth note of the following measure.

5) Corrected on the basis of the composer's instructions. The MS and Belyaev's edition give *a* sharp here.

6) Corrected on the basis of the MS. Belyaev and the other editions give *g* sharp.

7) Corrected on the basis of the MS. Belyaev and the other editions give *e* sharp.

Etudes: Op. 8 (Part I), No. 1

№ 2

A capriccio, con forza ♩=92

1) *mf* (according to the composer's instructions).

Etudes: Op. 8 (Part I), No. 2

Etudes: Op. 8 (Part I), No. 2

2) *p* }
3) — — — } (according to the composer's instructions).

Etudes: Op. 8 (Part I), No. 2

№ 3

Tempestoso ♩=80-92

1) The composer himself was not satisfied with this designation, since he did not think it fully corresponded to the character of the etude.

2) *rit.* (according to the composer's instructions).

3) - - - (according to the composer's instructions).
4) The composer thought it possible to begin this *dim.* a measure earlier, omitting the preceding *cresc.*
5) See note 3.

Etudes: Op. 8 (Part I), No. 3

6) According to the composer's instructions, a *cresc.* in this measure and a *subito* **p** in the next.

Etudes: Op. 8 (Part I), No. 3

7) See note 3.

№ 4

Piacevole ♩=100

1) *pp*
2) *accel.*
3) *rit.*
} according to the composer's instructions.

* In the MS and in Belyaev's edition:

5) *mp* }
6) *pp* } according to the composer's instructions.

7) According to the composer's instructions, the notes marked — should be slightly emphasized.

8) *pp*
9) *accel.* } according to the composer's instructions.
10) *rit.* }
11) See note 7.

Etudes: Op. 8 (Part I), No. 4

№ 5

Brioso ♩ = 72

mf semplice

cresc.

dim.

1) The original tempo designation was *Allegro.* Then the composer crossed out *Allegro* in the MS and put down *Brioso.* But this later designation did not satisfy him, either; he thought later on that it did not correspond to the character of the etude.

2) *p* }
3) --- } according to the composer's instructions.

Etudes: Op. 8 (Part I), No. 5

4) *accel.* (according to the composer's instructions).

5) In the MS and in Belyaev's edition:

6) Thus in the MS and in Belyaev's edition, but possibly this is a slip and should be: or:

7) *p*

8) *pp* according to the composer's instructions.

9)

Etudes: Op. 8 (Part I), No. 5

№ 6

Con grazia ♩.= 44

1) ♩ ♩ ♩ (according to the composer's instructions).

2) See note 1.

3) *p*
4) *port.* } (according to the composer's instructions).

* In the MS and in Belyaev's edition:

5) *port.* and *rit.* (according to the composer's instructions).

* In the MS and in Belyaev's edition:

Etudes: Op. 8 (Part I), No. 6

№ 7

Presto tenebroso, agitato ♪(♩.) = 132

Etudes: Op. 8 (Part II), No. 7

1) The MS has a *p* here.

Etudes: Op. 8 (Part II), No. 7

Tempo I

Etudes: Op. 8 (Part II), No. 7

№ 8

Lento (Tempo rubato) ♩=52

Poco più vivo ♩=66

rubato

1) *pp* (according to the composer's instructions).
2) The dynamic nuances in this passage, according to the
composer's instructions, are:

Etudes: Op. 8 (Part II), No. 8

Tempo I

3) See note 1.

4) *cresc.*
5) *p* } according to the composer's instructions.
6) See note 1.

7) - - -
8) *pp* } according to the composer's instructions.
9) *calando*

№ 9

Alla ballata ♩ - 120 = 136

sotto voce

1) Thus in the MS and in all editions. The composer himself, however, added a *b* here:

Etudes: Op. 8 (Part II), No. 9

Etudes: Op. 8 (Part II), No. 9

2) Thus in the MS and in all editions. The composer himself, however, added a g sharp here:

3) *accel.* (according to the composer's instructions).

4) **pp** (according to the composer's instructions).

Etudes: Op. 8 (Part II), No. 9

5) *p* (according to the composer's instructions).

Etudes: Op. 8 (Part II), No. 9

6) Thus in the MS and in all editions. The composer himself, however, added a g sharp here. See note 2.

7) A big *cresc.* in this measure (according to the composer's instructions).

8) According to the composer's instructions, this passage in the right hand, which is all but

unplayable, should be performed as:

Etudes: Op. 8 (Part II), No. 9

№ 10

1) *rit.* (composer's instructions).

* The MS has a 🎵 ✱ here.

Etudes: Op. 8 (Part II), No. 10

2) **pp** (composer's
   instructions).
3) See note 2.

4) According to the composer's instructions, this passage should be performed:

5) *pp* (according to the composer's instructions).

Etudes: Op. 8 (Part II), No. 10

6) *rit.* (according to the composer's instructions).
7) The notes marked — should be emphasized (composer's instructions).
8) See note 6.

Etudes: Op. 8 (Part II), No. 10

Etudes: Op. 8 (Part II), No. 10

№ 11

1) Andante cantabile ♩ = 63

1) Originally there was no tempo indication in the MS, and only *cantabile* appeared. Later *Andante* was added by Scriabin.

2) Originally this passage was written: Then the fifth sixteenth note (*d* flat) was deleted.

3) The composer considered a caesura necessary before this measure.

Etudes: Op. 8 (Part II), No. 11

4) According to the composer's instructions, these chords should be played *tenuto*.

№ 12

5) At the end of this measure the MS has a *dim.* which extends through the entire following measure and leads into the *pp*. However, the composer himself thought it was possible for this passage to have different dynamics: in place of the *dim.* he allowed a *cresc.* followed by *subito pp*, accompanying the latter with a *rit.* Then a *pp* is necessary at the beginning of this passage.

6) The MS has a *pp* here.

1) The MS has a *fp* here.

2) The fingering is based on the MS.

Etudes: Op. 8 (Part II), No. 12

Etudes: Op. 8 (Part II), No. 12

Etudes: Op. 8 (Part II), No. 12

Etudes: Op. 8 (Part II), No. 12

Etudes: Op. 8 (Part II), No. 12

3) In the MS the dynamics of the ending
are altogether different, namely:

Eight Etudes, Op. 42 (1903)

№ 1

Etudes: Op. 42, No. 1

Etudes: Op. 42, No. 1

205

Etudes: Op. 42, No. 1

prestissimo

Etudes: Op. 42, No. 1

№ 2

Etudes: Op. 42, No. 2

№ 3

Prestissimo ♩ = 76

Etudes: Op. 42, No. 3

Etudes: Op. 42, No. 3

№ 4

Andante ♩ = 60

Etudes: Op. 42, No. 4

Etudes: Op. 42, No. 4

№ 5

Affannato ♩=84

Etudes: Op. 42, No. 5

Etudes: Op. 42, No. 5

Etudes: Op. 42, No. 5

Etudes: Op. 42, No. 5

221

Etudes: Op. 42, No. 5

№ 6

Etudes: Op. 42, No. 6

Etudes: Op. 42, No. 6

Etudes: Op. 42, No. 6

№ 7

Etudes: Op. 42, No. 7

№ 8

Etudes: Op. 42, No. 8

poco cresc.

mf

Etudes: Op. 42, No. 8

Etudes: Op. 42, No. 8

Etudes: Op. 42, No. 8

Etude, Op. 49, No. 1 (1905)

Etudes: Op. 49, No. 1

Etude, Op. 56, No. 4 (1908)

Etudes: Op. 56, No. 4

Three Etudes, Op. 65 (1911–1912)

№ 1

Allegro fantastico ♪.=144–160

Agitato

Meno vivo ♩.= 50

dolciss.

pp *très doux avec langueur*

legato

m.d.

pochiss. cresc.

Etudes: Op. 65, No. 1

238

Tempo I

poco agitato

Etudes: Op. 65, No. 1

Etudes: Op. 65, No. 1

Etudes: Op. 65, No. 1

Ossia:

Poco agitato

Meno vivo

poco cresc.

Etudes: Op. 65, No. 1

Etudes: Op. 65, No. 1

№ 2

Etudes: Op. 65, No. 2

№ 3

Etudes: Op. 65, No. 3

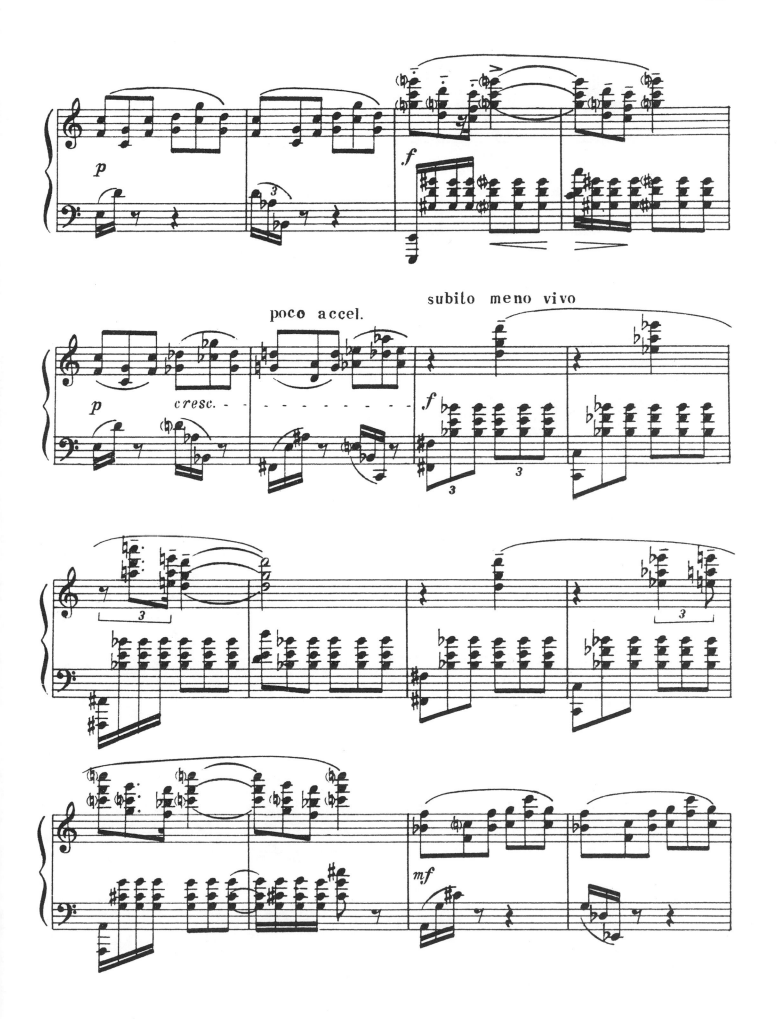

poco accel.

subito meno vivo

Etudes: Op. 65, No. 3

Etudes: Op. 65, No. 3

Etudes: Op. 65, No. 3